Nocita Carter

Dating Tips For You

ISBN-13: 978-0-9823485-2-9
ISBN-10: 0-9823485-2-5
Library of Congress Control Number: 2010921548

Disclaimer

Dating Tips For You is an informational book and does not assume any responsibility for errors contradictory interpretation of the information provided, subject material or omissions. The author and the publisher will have no liability or responsibility directly or indirectly to any person or entity in reference to any losses or damages that may arise from the tips and information provided in this book. In addition, this book is sold with the understanding that the author and publisher are not offering legal or psychological advice.

Published by WebLinks LLC
P.O. Box 892125
Temecula, CA. 92589-2125
www.books-from-weblinks.com

Table of Contents

Acknowledgements

Dating Tips For You is dedicated to anyone who would like to learn more about dating. If you have been wondering whether or not you should consider dating your coworker, neighbor, friend, someone special or about staying safe while you date and more, then the tips in this book are dedicated to you. You are the inspiration for me writing this book and it is hoped that the tips and information you read in this book will help you when you date that special someone you're interested in.

Thank you for your interest in this literary work and may you continue to enjoy more of the books published by WebLinks. Our books are created with you in mind.

Introduction

Ever thought about dating or going on a date but not really sure what you should do? Well, that's why this book was created to assist you in your quest to date.

Dating tips you may want to consider using before, during and after your date. You may be unsure of what to do on your date or ways to approach your date. You may be looking for some assistance on what you should consider while you're dating.

The dating tips presented throughout **Dating Tips For You** may give you some ideas about dating. So, go ahead and start reading **Dating Tips For You** to obtain tips and information you may be able to use when you consider dating.

Should I Ask Someone On A Date?

Robert really likes Angela and has wanted to ask her out for a long time. He first noticed Angela at his local gym two months ago and was attracted to her from the start. Robert has wanted to ask Angela out on a date, but just doesn't know how to. He would really like to get to know Angela if he could.

Robert's situation is similar to many people who are interested in asking out someone special, but just don't know how. Here are some tips to help you ask someone out on a date:

Tip One

Get past your fear of being rejected by someone you may ask out on a date. If you fear that you may be rejected by someone you ask on a date, then you'll never make it to first base. You've got to start somewhere. So, go ahead ask the person you're interested in on a date. Do it now!

If you get an answer of yes for the date, that's great. If they say no by rejecting your request for a date, move on to your next potential date. Just because someone rejects you for a date, does not mean that the next person will. So pick your head up, and you'll get that date with someone special that deserves you and only you.

Tip Two

When you ask for a first date, try to avoid setting up your first date on a Friday or Saturday. These two nights are usually reserved for more serious dating. In other words, if you're just starting out dating, don't start on a Friday or Saturday night until you get more serious about the person you're dating.

You might want to consider going out on a Wednesday or Thursday. These days seem to be more flexible for people during the week. Try to avoid dates on Monday's if possible. Most people don't care for Monday's.

Tip Three

After approaching someone for a date, be specific when asking that person out for a date. For example, you could ask the person the following question: I'm interested in seeing a play at our local theater on either a Wednesday or Thursday would you be interested in attending? This question is an opportunity for your prospective date to have options on deciding if they want to go on the date with you and if so, they can choose the day they want to go on the date and other options such as meeting you at the theater, etc…

Tip Four

Consider when asking someone out for a date, that you give them a sufficient amount of time for the date to take place. You may want to schedule the date a week in advance. However, you can always go with your gut feeling at the time if you think your prospective date will want to set that date sooner.

Tip Five

The best way to ask a person out on a date is in person. You have the opportunity to see the person you want to date face to face and observe their body language and facial expressions.

Using some or all of these tips to assist you in asking for a date may help you from having no dates to having dates. Robert decided to ask Angela out on a date by using these tips and they have been a couple every since their first date. They found they have a lot in common and enjoy each other's company. Robert was glad he finally found the nerve to ask Angela on a date by using these tips. Angela was glad he did too.

Should I Pay For This Date Or Should the Person I Date Pay The Bill?

That depends on how you or your date may feel about paying for the date. It is amazing that the subject of who should pay for a date can cause a person to become apprehensive, nervous and have anxiety.

Just the idea that they have to think about who will pay for the date can keep them from dating. This is because they do not want to discuss this subject and would just rather skip the date all together than deal with this issue.

You may both be more comfortable with splitting the bill especially in the early stages of dating. Of course you'll want to discuss what may be comfortable for the both of you. You never know your date may be more comfortable with paying for your date. Even you may also want to do this as well.

Still not sure about what to do? Well you may want to think about using some of these tips to assist you:

Tip One

Consider splitting the bill. Remember, you may have just started dating and you really don't know each other that well. Neither person owes the other anything. Think of it as though, you're out with some of your friends or coworkers. Don't you normally split the bill when it comes? You probably do. So consider doing this on your date.

Tip Two

Think about paying the entire bill and consider suggesting that your date pick up the tab for the next date. This gives you a good reason among other things to go on another date.

Tip Three

Make it fun. Toss a coin to see who gets to pay the bill. The winner of the coin toss does not have to pay the bill.

Tip Four

Consider inviting your date to your home for a meal or to watch movies. You will not have a bill to think about splitting and this may make your date priceless. This could also give the two of you more quality time together.

Tip Five

Go on a date that does not require you to split the bill. Consider going to the beach, park or do some leisure walking together. This makes for a nice date with no bill attached. You can enjoy each others company, without worrying about who will pay for the bill at the end of the date.

Enjoy your date. That's the whole idea isn't it? Don't make the question of who should pay for our date, a problem or issue for you when you date. Just go with what you feel is comfortable at the time of your date. Be spontaneous, just let the date flow, and you'll see that your date will probably work out just fine.

Is It Okay To Say No I'm Not Interested In Having Sex On My Date?

Yes, yes and yes! Don't feel you're obligated to have sex or give it up to someone when you date. It's okay to say no, I'm really not interested in taking this date to that level. If the person you date cannot accept that answer, it means they're really not for you anyway and you need to move on. There's nothing wrong with making the decision to tell the person you date absolutely no. You'll be glad that you did this in the long run.

So, you probably want to know, I just don't feel comfortable just simply saying no to sex to the person I am dating. You're thinking that the person you date may not understand your resistance, reluctance or decision not to have sex when you are dating. How do I go about letting the person I am dating know that I am not interested in having sex with them or I am just not ready? You can consider some of these tips to let the person know how you feel:

Tip One

If there is an expectation from your date that you should have sex, let your date know how you feel about sex while you date. Let your date know your feelings concerning this if this becomes a topic of discussion between the two of you. Be honest, let your date know how you truly feel about this. You do not want any misconceptions about your true feelings later on down the line.

Tip Two

Having sex while you date may be against your religious beliefs. If this is the case, then let the person you date know this. Its okay to let your date know how you feel. If they have a problem with your decision, then you did not need to date them anyway.

Tip Three

Tell your date that you want to remain celibate until you get married. If this is how you feel, stick to it and don't be swayed.

Tip Four

If you are not comfortable having sex with your date due to the potential of you catching a sexually transmitted disease such as; HIV, AIDS, gonorrhea, herpes or syphilis, you should be able to be open with your date on your feelings about this issue.

Your health should be one of your primary concerns. It's important that you protect yourself and it is okay to abstain from sex while you date. Just be up front with the person you date about this.

Tip Five

If you're just not interested in having sex at all with your date just plain and simple, that's okay too. If the person you are dating broaches the subject of sex with you, just tell them you have no interest in having sex when you date. If this becomes and issue, then just move on. Remember its okay to say no.

Hopefully these tips will assist you in letting the person you date understand, your feelings and concerns about why you are saying no to having sex with them while you date. Having sex while you date is a huge step and cannot be taken lightly. It is also having mutual respect for each others feelings, beliefs and concerns.

You should be able to tell the person that you date your true feelings about this subject so it does not become an issue later on. If there is a problem with you saying no to sex to your date and they do not agree with how you feel, then it's time for you to move on. You have made the right choice to do this and you'll be glad that you made this decision because this is the way you truly feel.

Should I Date My Boss Or Coworker?

That's a million dollar question. Dating your coworker or boss, someone you see at least five days a week, eight hours or more a day, why not? Well, that depends if dating your coworker will create problems in the workplace for you. Probably not a good idea to date your boss or coworker, this may cause problems for you down the line.

Imagine, you're in the company cafeteria talking to your coworker that you date. Sally and John just walked into the cafeteria and they immediately start staring and whispering to themselves about the two of you. You know they're talking about you because they look in your direction continuously while they whisper.

You and the coworker you date, feel very uncomfortable with Sally and John's reaction to you having lunch together. You think to yourselves that it may have been a mistake for you to have lunch together in the cafeteria where you work. You're now going to be the topic of your other coworkers' conversation you believe, thanks to Sally and John who are known in the workplace as the king and queen of gossiping at your job. Both of you now wonder if you should be dating and what you both were thinking when you decided to have lunch together in the company's cafeteria.

What type of problems could dating your coworker or maybe your boss cause? Well, what if you get into an argument at home or while you are on a date, when you go back to work you have to see that person almost everyday. If that person is your boss, then you could possibly loose that promotion you worked so hard for or maybe you have to walk on eggshells while you're at work. This could make you feel very uncomfortable.

Or, if you're getting along well with the coworker or boss you're dating, your coworkers may think when they see you together that you may be getting special treatment. Especially if the boss you are dating favors you and gives you a promotion. This may cause problems for both of you in the workplace.

Dating Tips For You

If you just have to date your coworker or boss, consider keeping your personal relationship outside of the workplace. When you participate in this type of relationship, keep it professional in the office and personal outside of the workplace. This is key in keeping the work place rumor mill to a minimum on having information about you and your coworker dating.

Only you will know if dating your coworker or boss will be a good idea for you. If you don't believe this will cause a problem, then go for it. There are many people that have found their soul mates in the workplace. So do what makes you happy, after all you are in control of your own destiny and your love life.

I Want To Date My Neighbor Should I?

Jason just moved to his new home two months ago. He is still ecstatic about getting his new home in the neighborhood he always wanted to live in. He's a marketing executive with his company and has worked for them for over five years. Jason has met most of his neighbors and they all seem very friendly and easy to get along with.

There is one neighbor that lives across the street that he has not met. But, he is anxious to do so, because he noticed that this neighbor is very attractive and seems to be someone he would like to know better. He's seen his attractive neighbor at least three times from a distance and definitely likes what he sees.

Jason would like to meet his attractive neighbor, but, he wants to make sure he makes a good first impression. He wants to literally make his neighbor like him from the very start. He's been working on how he should approach her or maybe he thought he shouldn't approach her at all. He's really not sure.

He knows if he doesn't impress his neighbor that he is interesting, he'll have to deal with seeing her across the street from his home. Jason faces a dilemma on what he should do. Should he consider asking his neighbor out? Maybe, Jason could consider doing some of the following tips:

Tip One
Go for it Jason! You'll never know if your neighbor will like you well enough to go on a date if you don't ask her out. Just make sure you don't seem overly anxious when you approach your neighbor. Don't embarrass yourself.

Tip Two
Maybe consider introducing yourself to your neighbor first. Then consider at a later time, when you've had the opportunity to assess your neighbor to determine whether or not you really want to go out on a date. You may find from your initial conversation with your neighbor that the neighbor may look good but you really do not seem to have anything in common with your neighbor.

Tip Three

Consider volunteering to do something around your neighbor's home to get the opportunity to find out whether or not this person may be someone you want to go on a date with. You'd be amazed at how much information you may get about this person on that particular occasion. You get a chance to test the waters so to speak.

Tip Four

You may want to consider not dating your neighbor at all. You would probably alleviate possible future problems down the line if dating your neighbor just doesn't work out.

Tip Five

Consider giving yourself more time to settle into your home before you approach your neighbor about going on a date. This will give you a period of time to find out if this is really what you want and should do.

So, Jason may want to think real hard about asking his neighbor out on a date. He may want to introduce himself first to his neighbor and take his time before he takes that leap to ask his neighbor on a date. He'll be glad he did in the long run. As a matter of fact, anyone thinking about dating they're neighbor, may want to consider these same tips that Jason is also thinking about.

Can I Date To Have Fun With No Commitment?

So you say you just want to date to have fun with no strings attached. Well, that's okay if you want to do this as long as the person you're dating is on the same page as you are. There will probably be no problem if you both already understand that you can have open dating in your relationship.

If you have not communicated your decision to have carefree open dating with the person you're dating, then this may be a problem for you. What is the best way to tell someone that you don't want to be committed to them when dating? You may want to consider the following tips:

Tip One
Let the person you're dating know right from the beginning that you want no commitment to

them and would like to date other people. Tell the person you're dating that this is a two way street and they can also date other people as well. It's best to set the record straight right from the beginning so there is no misunderstanding. If the person you're dating wants a commitment and does not want an open relationship then you'll both know this from the very start and you can both go your own separate ways.

Tip Two

You may want to consider going on dates with different people on different days of the week as part of your non commitment plan. You may even consider dating on a weekly, biweekly or monthly basis different people. Yeah that's right, this may even add a little or a lot of spice to your dating life.

Tip Three

Not being committed to dating someone gives you the opportunity to date and meet many different people. For instance, if you were at a restaurant and met someone you may want to consider dating, you could ask them out right then and there. Remember you don't commit to dating one particular person, so you're open and free to do this.

22

So, as you can see there are different ways to be uncommitted to dating. It has its advantages and disadvantages. Of course, this all depends on you and what it is you're seeking to do when you date someone. It's really up to you. You can have the opportunity to meet lots of people and have more choices of who you may ultimately want to be with. You may find that in the long run that you'll eventually meet your soul mate during your dating span.

Of course a disadvantage to being uncommitted when you're dating is that the person you may be considering to date, may not be interested in an open relationship where there is no commitment. That means you loose out on dating the person you may be interested in dating. So, only you can decide on what type of dating you'd like to pursue. Just make sure you're comfortable with the choice you have made and that it is the right choice for you.

Should My Date Meet My Family and Friends?

If you're letting your date meet your family and friends you must be getting more serious about the person you're dating. That's good. You may be a little apprehensive about your date meeting your family and friends because you want things to go well.

You want your friends and family to like the person you date and your date to like them. Don't worry about it. Just be yourselves and move forward with the introductions. Here are some tips and information that may help you when you're preparing to have your date meet your family and friends:

Tip One

You may want to prepare your date for meeting your family by making them aware of any family traditions or what may be expected by your family. For example, if your family expects on Sundays that everyone in the family attend dinner at your parents home by 5:00 p.m., let the person you're dating know this.

Tip Two

Introduce your date to your friends. Yes that's right it's okay to see what your friends think about your date. Just don't hold your friends opinion to heart if they don't like the person you're dating. Ultimately it's your choice on how you feel about the person you're interested in.

Tip Three

Let your date know about certain family members and friends that may cause or have a prospective problem with your date. You know the family member or friend who does not think anyone you date is good enough for you and their attitude is usually very negative. Let your date know what to expect and that this would be normal behavior for that particular person. That way your date won't be surprised if your family or friend is negative towards them. This will hopefully ease a potential problem brewing for your date prior to them meeting people they don't know.

Tip Four

Make sure your date will be comfortable or is actually ready to meet your family and friends. If your date is not ready to meet your family and friends, then hold off on the introductions. You want to make sure that your date is ready to take that leap and you don't want to push them into doing something they're not prepared to do. Take it slow, you'll eventually get there. Remember, patience is a virtue.

Tip Five

Anything else you can think of to prepare your date to meet your family and friends. Just make sure your date is prepared to meet the other significant people in your life.

Meeting your family and friends can be an interesting and informative experience for your date. It can also be a challenge to your relationship that could possibly be a relationship ender. That's why it's important for you to give your date some background information on your family and friends. Think about the two of you, it's your relationship and you both must be happy with each other. So, follow your heart and both of you will make the right decision about each other before and after your date has met your family and friends.

What Should I Do If I Am Middle Aged or A Senior Citizen and I Want To Start Dating Again?

You should go for it! You're never too old to date. The hardest part of making the decision to start dating again is you deciding to begin the process of dating. You may be thinking that I'm over forty years old and who would be interested in dating me? Well, believe it or not, there are many people that would be interested in dating you. You just need to get the ball rolling again.

It does not matter if you are single, have never married, divorced, widow or are a widower, you can still date if you're middle aged or a senior citizen. Remember most people are living longer so you still have your life ahead of you. You say you don't have a clue of where to start when it comes to dating. Well, consider some of these tips when you prepare to start dating:

Tip One

Get past your fear of being rejected by someone you may ask out on a date. If you fear that you may be rejected by someone you ask on a date, then you'll never make it to first base. You've got to start somewhere.

So, go ahead ask the person you're interested in on a date. Do it now, you probably will not regret taking that step forward on asking someone special out on a date.

If you get an answer of yes for the date, that's great. If they say no by rejecting your request for a date, move on to your next potential date. Just because someone rejects you for a date, does not mean that the next person will. So pick your head up, and you'll get that date with someone special who deserves you.

Tip Two

When you ask for a first date, try to avoid setting up your first date on a Friday or Saturday. These two nights are usually reserved for more serious dating. In other words, if you're just starting out don't start on a Friday or Saturday night until you get more serious about the person you're dating. You might want to consider going out on a Tuesday, Wednesday or Thursday. These days seem to be more flexible for people during the week.

Tip Three

After approaching someone for a date, be specific when asking that person out for a date. For example, you could ask the person the following question: I'm interested in seeing a movie at our local theater on either a Tuesday, Wednesday or Thursday would you be interested in going? This question is able to provide the opportunity for your prospective date to have options on deciding if they want to go on the date with you and if so, they can choose the day they want to go on the date and other options such as meeting you at the theater, restaurant, bowling alley, etc...

Tip Four

Consider when asking someone out for a date that you give them a sufficient amount of time for the date to take place. However, you can always go with your gut feeling at the time if you think your prospective date will want to set that date sooner.

Tip Five

The best way to ask a person out is in person. You have the opportunity to see the person you want to date face to face and observe their body language and facial expressions. This may also assist you in giving you more confidence and making you more comfortable when you date.

Tip Six

Consider a simple date. Going to a local park is a great date believe it or not. If you decide to go to a local park, take a picnic basket for lunch or dinner. You may want to take some music, games etc…with you to the park. I'm sure you can think of a few things that you and your date may enjoy while you are in the park. This will help you to get to know each other better.

Tip Seven

You may want to break the ice with you date, by meeting them for breakfast or even at another venue such as; a coffee house, juice bar, yogurt factory, etc…This may also assist in breaking the ice on your first date.

Tip Eight

Consider meeting your date at a local museum. That's right, this can be a great initial date. Going to a museum could be a great way to impress your date and could also be an informative experience for the both of you.

So, just be creative when you decide to get back into dating. Don't be hard on yourself, just get started. You will not have the potential to meet someone until you put your foot forward to get started. You'll be glad that you did, and you will probably wonder why it took you so long to get started.

I Want To Date Someone Who Is Married Should I?

Good question. But the answer is no. Absolutely not, unless you're looking for trouble in your relationship. Because there's bound to be problems later on down the line for you and the person who you're thinking about dating who is married. You're probably wondering why not take the chance and go for it. You're a person that likes challenges. Well a challenge is what you may get and possibly some additional problems along the way. So why bother taking the risk of future problems later on. What future problems could there be? Well you may run into some or all of these problems in the following tips:

Tip One
The spouse of the married person you're dating catches you out on a date when you least expect

it. This could be very embarrassing for the both of you. How would you like the spouse of the person you're currently dating to have an angry confrontation in front of the two of you in a public place that you are in at a particular time. The angry spouse may not only be verbally confrontational but may get physical with you as well. This would not be good for either of you nor the person's spouse.

Tip Two

Or maybe the relatives or friends of the person you are dating caught you both at a restaurant, movie, etc…together. How would you explain this to them or your spouse? This would be an awkward situation for the both of you.

Tip Three

For example, you or your date are at each others home while they're spouse is away on a business trip or at work. You get very comfortable in your date's home and the telephone rings while they're in the kitchen cooking dinner. You make the mistake of picking up the telephone and low and behold your date's spouse is on the phone wondering why you answered they're telephone. Are you going to be able to explain yourself? Probably not.

Tip Four

You decided to purchase flowers for your date because you like him or her and are trying to make a good impression. You forget and used the joint credit card that you have with your spouse to pay for the flowers. Your wife or husband just happened to get home early from work one day and they went to the mailbox instead of you. Guess what? They got the credit card statement out of the mailbox that shows the charges you made for those flowers for your date. You're confronted by your spouse who has evidence that you've been cheating on them.

Tip Five

You decide to let your boyfriend who is also married borrow your new candy red sports car to run some errands he has before your date in the evening. Your husband is away on a business trip. You received your new shiny red sports car from your husband for your birthday two months ago. Just so happen, your husband arrived home from his business trip early and decided that he would surprise you. As he turned into the driveway of your home, your boyfriend was exiting your driveway at the same time your spouse arrived. Your spouse was furious to see another man driving the vehicle he just recently purchased for you. Your boyfriend sped out of your driveway when he saw that it was your husband and crashed into an oncoming vehicle. You got busted and not only did your spouse catch you, but now you have to deal with the accident that your boyfriend had with your new car.

So, see how dating someone who is married is not a good idea. This could create lots of problems for not only the two of you, but the people who may be in relationships with the both of you. Your relationship could also have a negative impact on your children and other family members as well. The best policy is just don't do it.

What Should I Not Tell My Date?

Yes, some things you shouldn't tell the person you're dating because it's really not important. Some things are best left unsaid. You wouldn't want to turn off the person you're dating to the point they determine they're really not interested in you after all. So, here are some tips that may assist you in not discussing certain topics with your date that your date does not need to know:

Tip One

Never discuss with your date your past boyfriend, girlfriend or former spouse. This is a definite no, no. No one wants to hear about how great or bad your past girlfriend, boyfriend, or former spouse was. Don't dwell on the past. Your new date may think you're carrying a lot of negative baggage about your prior girlfriend, boyfriend or former spouse. This may end up being a turn off for the person you want to date.

Tip Two

Don't talk about how much money you have or lack of it. This may come across to your date as your way of telling them that money is the most important thing to you in a relationship. This could be a relationship ender for you.

Tip Three

Do not gossip about your past dates, friends, family or whoever, this is not a good idea. It's really not important for you to discuss this with your date. Some people see others that gossip as busy bodies who have to be involved in everyone elses business but their own. This may be a turnoff for your date who could be a person that values their privacy and is a non gossiper.

Tip Four

Don't discuss your past intimate relationships. This is a definite no for discussion. This may make your date very uncomfortable and put them in an awkward position as to what you may or may not expect from them. So don't discuss your past intimacies. Steer far away from this topic. Don't even talk about it. This would be your best bet in your new relationship if you don't want to create waves.

Tip Five

If you cheated on your previous date, don't even think about talking about this in your new relationship. No one wants to hear about you cheating in a past relationship. If you decide to talk about this subject, be prepared for your date to possibly tell you to take a hike. They may decide that they don't want to risk the chance of you cheating on them, since you have a history of doing this. Get the picture, don't talk about it.

Tip Six

Anything else that you believe would not be something important that you'd want to tell your date about you. Don't tell it, if it's not important.

Well, you probably have a good idea on what you should not tell your date. After all, do you want to keep dating the person you're with, or do you want to keep looking for someone new? You're possibly saying to yourself, I really would like to continue dating the person I'm with. Then, if this is the case, don't scare them away from you. Remember, some things are best left unsaid if the information is not important to the relationship.

I Have Kids, Should I Tell My Date?

Yes, yes, and yes! Let your date know you have kids on your first date. If your date can't accept the fact that you have kids then this is a red flag that you should not go on any future dates with this person. Your kids are part of who you are, if your date has a problem with this then they have a problem with you.

Kenneth says to himself, I really like Sharon, and I know she is single and has no kids because I overheard her tell her trainer Irene at the gym that she doesn't. I really want to ask her out on a date, but I have four kids that I'm raising on my own and I don't think she'll like me when she finds out. I'm not sure what I should do.

Sharon says to herself, there's this guy I met at the gym his name is Kenneth. I really like him, he always seems to know the right things to say and is so polite. I really would like to go out with him. I just don't think he'll go out with me. I'm feeling guilty because I lied to my trainer Irene the other day and told her that I don't have any kids. I actually have three children. I told Irene this out loud so Kenneth could hear what I said and maybe he might want to date me. I'm not sure what I should do now. I would really like to go out with Kenneth, I just don't know how I should tell him about my kids. How do I go about telling my date about my kids? You can tell your date about your kids by using some of these tips:

Tip One

During your date while making conversation, let your date know you have children. Also take the opportunity to find out if your date has children as well. You should know whether or not the person you date is comfortable with you having children. If not, then consider yourself lucky you found out right away so you can move on to someone else that appreciates you and your kids as one complete package.

Tip Two

If you correspond with your date via telephone or email prior to seeing each other in person, let your date know you have kids. You say, I told my date that I have kids and they don't want to go on another date with me, what should I do? Do nothing, consider yourself lucky that you found out that your date does not like kids. You didn't need to be with that person anyway. Good ritenance to them. Just move on. Date someone who will accept you and your kids, that's more important. You will be glad you found out sooner rather that later about your date.

The sooner you let your date know you have kids the sooner you can get past this issue if it becomes a problem. The whole idea of dating is to date someone you are compatible with and who will want you for who you are and it should not matter whether or not you have children. Remember your children will always be a part of you and they are truly a blessing to you. So, it is okay to move on to someone else who will appreciate you and your children.

How Do We Get Our Conversation Started On Our Date?

That's good, you've made it to first base. The effort you took to get this date has paid off, and now you need help on what you should say to keep the person interested. Well, you could try some of these tips that may help you get your conversation started:

Tip One

Always and foremost, be yourself. Don't fake who you are or pretend you're someone you're not. This will certainly catch up with you later. Being yourself on your date is the best way to go. The person you are seeing gets to see the real you. They can decide if they're going to continue to be interested in you or not. If they are still interested that's good. If not, that's okay too. Just move on to someone who will like you for you.

Tip Two

Break the ice by introducing yourself and providing information about yourself that you feel comfortable letting someone know about you. You could tell your date about your hobbies, occupation, movies or games you would like to see and play, and other interests that you may have.

Tip Three

Smile. That's right, smile sometimes with your date. This can help you and your date to release nervous tension you may have built up before and during your date. Smiling helps you to relax and become more comfortable with each other. So go ahead, try it! It won't hurt. Your date will probably love your beautiful or handsome smile.

Tip Four

Get comfortable with your date by considering being creative to assist in keeping the conversation going between the two of you. Maybe, you and your date can pick a topic to discuss such as; current events, sports, movies or plays you have seen. This could make your conversation very interesting and you'll get to learn more about each other. Isn't that great? I thought so.

Tip Five

Remember your first impression to your date may be your last impression. So make sure you remain true to who you are and the person you're dating. If it is meant for you to be with the person you're dating, then you'll know. If not, you'll know you should move on to someone else. Just remember to put your best foot forward and remain honest. Not only will you keep your self respect, others including your date, will respect you too.

So, you've got some tips to assist you with what you can do to get the conversation started once you get your date. Go ahead, you can do it! Just start using some or all of these tips to help you to get your conversation started for your date.

Can I Get A Telephone Phone Number From Someone For A Possible Date?

Maybe yes, maybe no. That depends on if you're interested in going on a date with that person. You may not be sure at the time you meet the person whether or not you want to go on a date. If this is the case, you may want to consider taking their phone number for future reference. However, if you don't think you would be interested, then don't take their number. Some of these tips may help you decide whether or not you should take someone's phone number:

Tip One
You want to call the person so you can talk with them and consider going on a date. So you

may want to get your prospective date's telephone number.

Tip Two

If you're not sure about whether or not you want to call the person, take their phone number if you're not totally sure. This may be your only opportunity.

Tip Three

Consider giving the person your telephone number. You may have the option of providing your home, cell phone or work number to the person you may consider dating. This may make the other person more comfortable and less pressured that they are not being asked to give out their phone number to you. By giving them your telephone number, the person has an option of whether or not they want to contact you.

Tip Four

After deciding to get a person's telephone number, remember men and women are different when it comes to calling each other. Men may want to take a longer period of time to call a woman than the woman may expect it to take. Women may expect that when a man receives their telephone number they should call them soon after meeting them. It's okay for the woman to call the man after initially meeting him instead of waiting for him to do so. Go with how you feel about this.

Tip Five

Make sure if you're not interested in the person, don't give out your telephone number you may regret it later. Just say no, in a polite way if you're not interested in the person. That's okay. That gives that person and you the opportunity to move on to someone else they may be interested in.

Getting a person's telephone number may or may not be easy. It just depends on whether or not you or that person may be interested in each other. It is important to remember that collecting a telephone number of no substance is totally different than obtaining a telephone number from someone special that you may be able to have a future connection with. So make sure when you get their phone number, you really want it, and the person giving it to you wants you to have it.

What Should I Tell My Date?

Good question? When you first start dating it's important to tell the person you're dating important information about yourself before you get too deep into the relationship. You say, well isn't my name, occupation, hobbies and telephone number enough? No, not if you're withholding information from the other person you're dating.

The information you need to tell your date may be important to that person in deciding whether or not they want to remain in a relationship with you. It's best to let them know about you right from the start. You don't want this to become a problem for you later on down the line.

If the person you're dating chooses not to continue dating you, then move on to someone else that you may want to date. That way, you will both be happier. So, you want to know what types

Nocita Carter

of things you should let your date know about you,
here are some tips and information that may assist
you with this:

Tip One

Let your date know that you have children.
Most people don't have a problem with their date
having children. You may find in most cases that
your date may have kids themselves and may not be
sure how to approach this subject as well. So why
not tell your date. It's good to let your date know
early on if you have children. There are some people that don't want to date someone with children.
If this is the case with your date, then they've found
out early from you, that you have kids and you can
both move on to someone else. Go ahead, get if off
your chest, you'll feel glad that you did.

Tip Two

Let your date know if you have a criminal record. Yes, your date should know if you've spent
time in jail for a crime you've committed. You say
you've done your time, why does my date need
to know this information? They need to know because, this may come out in the relationship at a
later time when you least expect it, especially if
you're on probation. How would you explain to

someone you're dating that you need to meet with your parole officer after your date just happened to take a phone message from your probation officer while you were busy in your kitchen cooking a romantic dinner for the both of you. Oops! See how awkward that would be for you. Be up front, let your date know about your criminal history if you have one.

Tip Three
If you have bad credit let your date know about your credit history. If you've been dating for awhile and you're getting serious about each other, let your date know that your credit isn't good. This will eliminate surprises for you and your date if you decide that you want a long term relationship. Your date will know that your credit is not so perfect.

Tip Four
Tell your date if you're unable to have children or just don't want to have any kids. Let your date know about this early on when you start dating. If your date wants children, they will have a choice to exit the relationship with you early on. You will also have the same opportunity because you would have found out that your date may want children and you may not.

Tip Five

Tell your date about any health problems that you may have that would affect your relationship. It's important that you reveal to the person you're dating any health problems you have so they can decide early on if they will be able to handle this as part of your relationship. If they can't, then move on to someone else who does not have a problem with this. Remember, there's always other fish in the sea that will accept you for who you are.

Tip Six

Anything else you believe is important for your date to know about you before you get too deep into your relationship.

By providing your date with important information about you, this gives them a choice to determine whether or not they will continue dating you. More important, you're being honest in the relationship. In addition, it shows that not only do you respect yourself, you take responsibility by being forthright with respecting others rights to make their own choice about whether or not they want to be with you in a relationship.

Where Can I Meet Someone To Date?

Good question. You know there are lots of places you could meet someone you'd like to date. What's important here is that you don't limit yourself on where you can meet someone. Go with how you feel, and if it feels right to you at that moment, then go for it! What do you have to loose?

Jackie was down in the dumps because she hadn't met anyone since her break-up with Matthew six months ago. She had dated Matthew for almost two years and they decided to go their own separate ways because they felt after two years they really weren't compatible. They also discovered that their marriage goals were different.

Jackie wasn't ready to settle down and have kids and Matthew was ready to get married and start a family. So, they decided to go their own separate ways. Jackie was alone and with no one. She was depressed and didn't know what she was going to do. Her friend Monica decided to help Jackie with her quest of trying to find out where she could meet someone to date. So, Monica started looking for information to help Jackie find a place to meet someone and low and behold, she ran across these tips and information to assist her friend in meeting someone. Monica also found this information helpful to her as well. You may want to consider some of these tips when you are trying to meet someone special:

Tip One

Consider your favorite hobbies or things you like to do when trying to find someone to meet for a date. You will probably find that this will lead you to a place that you can meet someone to date. For example, if you like going to concerts, you may want to book a ticket to a concert and this will provide you with a venue to meet someone.

Or, if you like reading, go to your favorite bookstore to pick up a book and maybe you'll meet someone special. Get the idea? By using your hobby or what you like to do, this could lead you in the direction of meeting someone you may want to date.

Tip Two

Make a connection through a dating service to meet someone. There are many dating services to choose from these days. In fact, you can join dating services via the internet or off line. So you may want to consider this source when you're trying to meet someone to date.

Tip Three

Social events are a good way to meet someone. Some of these social events would include the following: festivals, private parties, parades, sporting functions and other types of events. At these particular events there are multitudes of people in attendance, so the possibility of meeting someone is practically endless.

Tip Four

Various clubs are a good source for meeting people, such as; health fitness clubs, professional clubs, comedy clubs, night clubs, and any other types of clubs you can think of which would be of interest to you in meeting someone.

Tip Five

If you like fun in the sun, consider amusement parks, beaches, and maybe the zoo. If you like it inside, consider going to a video arcade where you can meet someone who's interested in video games like you. You could also consider going to a museum.

Tip Six

Hey what about the mall, supermarket or hardware store? Yeah, that's right. These are great places to meet people. Maybe you like to shop, or possibly don't really have a choice, then why not consider meeting that special someone you may want to date at the supermarket or mall. You never know if you will meet your prince or princess on aisle nine where your favorite bread is located in the supermarket.

Tip Seven

Movie theaters are also good places to meet someone you may want to date. As you already probably know, lots of people go to the movies on a daily basis so you may catch the love of your life there. Go ahead, try it.

Tip Eight

Business seminars and conventions are also good places to meet someone as well. I know you're probably saying, hey I'm on business this isn't a social trip. Well, that's okay. There's nothing wrong with mixing business with pleasure. I'm sure you'll have some down time after your business is completed to mingle and chat with other business associates attending the seminar or convention. This is a perfect opportunity to meet that someone special.

Tip Nine

Why not at work, if you're comfortable meeting someone at your workplace that you may consider dating. It may not necessarily be a person working for the same company you're working for, it could be someone who works at another company in the same office building.

Tip Ten

Consider your friends and relatives as a source for meeting someone you may want to date. You never know your friend or relative may know someone that you can make a love connection with.

So, as you can see there are lots of places and opportunities you can meet someone you may want to date. You can probably think of more places to

Nocita Carter

meet someone yourself in addition to the tips listed here. So go ahead get started, pick a place you can meet someone and you may eventually meet the right person to date.

Should I Ask My Friend Out On A Date?

Possibly yes, possibly no, this depends on the relationship you have with your friend. Will asking your friend out make them uncomfortable? Or, is it that you both feel the same way but don't know how to approach each other about this subject.

You say, you don't want to ruin the relationship you have with your friend, if you ask them out for a date and they say no. You couldn't deal with the rejection and embarrassment that you may feel later on.

Sandra has known Tom for three years and they are close friends. Tom's had a crush on Sandra for the last two years but does not know how to let Sandra know how he feels. Ironically, Sandra has wanted to date Tom since they met while attending college classes three years ago. She has wanted Tom to ask her out on a formal date, but he hasn't.

She even thought about asking him out, but she was unsure if this would create problems for their friendship. Neither one of them knows what they should do, so they haven't done anything about how they feel about each other.

Could it be that your friend is feeling the same way you do, but also has a fear of rejection as well. There's got to be an easier way to break the ice, to get us both past this, if we think our relationship can be more than a friendship.

Are there some signs that you both are giving off that may make you think you are attracted to each other in a romantic way outside of your friendship? Well, here are some signs that you may want to look for, when you consider approaching your friend about going on a date and developing a possible romantic relationship:

Sign One
You both enjoy spending lots of time together and never seem to get enough of each other.

Sign Two
Both of you find yourselves staring at each other for long periods of time but don't say how you feel about each other romantically.

Sign Three

You both spend almost everyday with each other and you feel like no day is complete without spending time together.

Sign Four

Both of you feel butterflies inside when you see each other and are very anxious and happy to be together.

Sign Five

You and your friend think about each other all the time. You both find that you say each others names all the time. You even sometimes complete each others sentences.

Well, if you and your friend have any of these signs then it sounds like you're more than just good friends. You must be in love. It's probably a good idea at this point to go for it! Ask your friend out on a date. Chances are, your friend may have wanted to do the same thing. You'll be happy you did. Both of you will probably wonder why you didn't do this sooner. Looks like Sandra and Tom will be asking each other out on a date soon.

When Should I Not Date?

Very good question. There are actually times when you should consider not dating anyone. Why, you may be wondering can't I date someone whenever I want to? Well, there are various times in a person's life that involving someone in your own personal issues or problems is not a good idea. In fact, this may create problems for the person you are trying to date. You may be wondering what instances you would not want to consider dating someone. These tips will assist you in deciding whether or not you should date someone:

Tip One
You're married! Absolutely out of the question for you to decide that you want to date. Married means you're committed to someone else and you should be off limits to freely date. Remember you're not single anymore. So, don't even think about dating. This would be totally unfair to the person you're married too.

Tip Two

Just recently divorced. You may want to consider holding off on dating until you get readjusted to single life and your new status of now being unmarried and on your own. Once you give yourself enough time to readjust, preferably at least one year, then go for it! Start dating if you want to.

Tip Three

Lost your job and place to live because of your reduced or no income. There are a lot of people that are living together because they don't have a home or job. So, the person they're dating may decide to let the other person live with them. This is not a good idea and is not a good reason to date someone.

Big mistake and most couples regret this later. In most of these situations, the person that supports the person not working and without a home, begins to have resentment. They feel taken advantaged of and used because they are now the primary bread winner for the person they are dating who is no longer working. Often in these situations, the couple does not really know each other. They actually started living together after only a few dates. Consider giving the person you're dating another alternative of having some where else to stay instead of with you.

Tip Four

You're already dating someone you've been with for a long time. Don't date someone else if you're not willing to break off your relationship with your present girlfriend or boyfriend. You can play the field, but, let the person you've been dating know that you want to branch out and they can too. If you're not ready to do this, then don't start trying to date someone else.

Tip Five

You've just lost a loved one. It's difficult when you've lost someone you loved. So, you may want to consider waiting awhile before you start dating someone else. It takes time for your heart to start healing. You'll need time to yourself for awhile before you bring someone else into your life to date. This would not only be fair to you, but to the person you plan on dating in the future.

There are other instances that I'm sure you can think of when knowing whether or not you should start dating. Only you will know this. Dating for most people is considered an important element of their lives. When choosing to date, just remember the responsibility you have to yourself and others to ensure that you're doing the right thing,

Nocita Carter

at the right time, and what will ultimately make you happy and feel good without creating problems for yourself and others along the way.

Staying Safe When Meeting Someone On A Date

Carol just finished her online chat with David who she met online a couple of months ago. They chatted online for at least two hours a day and seemed to have similar interests. Carol thought to herself that David may be her soul mate, but they have never met each other in person. So, prior to the end of Carol's internet chat session with David this time, he asked her if he could meet her tomorrow night at her home. This question took Carol off guard and she did not really know how to respond to David. Her first mind told her that she should not meet David at her home. He was a stranger to her and she did not know him other than chatting with him over the internet.

She hesitated for a few minutes to David's question and she made a decision reluctantly to al-

Nocita Carter

low David to come to her home to meet her for the very first time. Carol now has apprehensions about making such a quick decision to allow David to come to her home. She now wished that she had made a better decision and does not know what she should do now.

So, it seems that Carol is in an awkward position at this time concerning what she should do about David visiting her home. Carol may want to consider these tips that may be able to assist her in staying safe when meeting someone on a date:

Tip One
If you make a quick or rash decision like Carol has, it should not be too late to correct your decision. It would be a good idea to call the person back and let them know that you would like to meet in a public place where you both would probably feel more comfortable since you are just meeting each other. That way, you are upfront with the person you are meeting for your date which may eliminate awkwardness, being uncomfortable and any problems that may potentially arise.

Tip Two
You may want to suggest a public place to meet for your date that could include: restaurant, coffee

house, museum, park, movie theater, bowling alley, etc...I think you get the picture.

Tip Three
Let a family member, friend or co-worker know information in reference to where, when and with whom you are going on a date with. This will assist with making you more comfortable with your date. It's important that you let someone close to you know about your date in case any potential problem arises.

Tip Four
Be careful about how much personal information you release about yourself to the person you date. Remember this person is a stranger and you do not know them. This is your first time meeting them so you will need to be careful about the information you provide to that person. You may consider releasing a small amount of information about yourself until you really have the opportunity to spend more time with your date. You want to be comfortable and assured that the person you are providing your personal information to is someone that really should be getting this information from you.

Nocita Carter

Staying safe when meeting someone on a date is important and will help you be able to really enjoy your date with having a comfortable piece of mind that you have attempted to take the precautions needed to enjoy your date by staying safe. You will be glad that you considered and followed through on some if not all of these tips to assist you with preparing and staying safe on your date. Just keep in mind, it's better to be proactive than reactive to any potential problems you may have while on a date with someone you do not know.

Conclusion

So you have finished reading this book **Dating Tips For You**. Now you're hopefully armed with more tips about dating that you can use when you date someone. The information provided in this book may make you more aware of dating tips you did not know. You may have considered some of these dating tips or just plain old forgot about them and just needed a refresher. Hopefully these dating tips will help you when you decide to go on a date with someone today, tomorrow or in your future dating.

About The Author

Nocita Carter has been writing for many years and resides in Temecula, California. Through my literary works I hope to provide tips and information on various topics to help others. This book was created for you.

Knowledge inspires those who hunger for more of it and a thirst that must be fulfilled for what they do not know and what they want to know more about. Remember by taking in and absorbing more information for yourself, you may be able to help others along the way with your expanded knowledge base. I look forward to writing more literary works that will inspire and help others along the way.

Index

www.ingramcontent.com/pod-product-compliance
Lightning Source LLC
Chambersburg PA
CBHW060132050426
42448CB00010B/2083